From Survival Jobs to your Dream Job

*How to **Transform** Your Resume, Cover Letter, and Interview Techniques to Get Your Dream Job **as a Nurse** Working Abroad, and **Invigorate your Life***

© 2019 Chester Gonzales. All Rights Reserved.
All rights reserved. No part of this book may be reproduced in any form without permission in writing from the author.

Disclaimer

The information contained in this book is based on personal experience and anecdotal evidence and is for educational purposes only. Although the author has made very reasonable attempt to achieve complete accuracy of the content of this product, he assumes no responsibility for errors or omissions.

You should use this information as you see fit and at your own risk. Everyone's situation is unique, and applying the information found on this book is no way guarantees employment or any other result desired form reading this book. The author assumes no responsibility or liability whatsoever on the behalf of the purchaser or reader of these materials.

foreignurse /ˈfôrənərs/

noun

A world-class nurse who chooses to work abroad for professional and personal growth; and despite the challenges of the profession, the migration and the circumstances, still able to give the best possible care to all types of client, with compassion and conviction.

www.foreignurse.com

To all the *foreignurses*.

The world needs nurses. You are an incredible being that through your care, you can change the world of an individual, a world of few or the entire world. Keep doing what you love. Once a nurse, always a nurse.

Table of Contents

Introduction 1

Part I: Creating your Business Card 3

Ten Tips to Transform your Resume so that it is Interesting for Prospective Employers 5

Part II: Elevating your Elevator Pitch 25

Three Tips for Effective Cover Letter Writing 27

Part III: Building Your Brand: Intervene in Interview Disasters 32

Three Most Common Disasters During Interview 34

Five Essential Things to Remember to Avoid Interview Disasters 39

Five Ways to Improve and Effectively Utilize Your Verbal Communication Skills in a Job Interview 42

Four Types of Healthcare Interview Questions 49

The 4 S in Answering Interview Questions that Builds your Brand .. 52

The Surest Way to Find a Job in Canada: My Powerful Six Tips 63

What Happens on Your First Day at Work in Canada? A Tale of All My Firsts in Canada 70

First Day with Pay — Pay per Work 71

First Day Working with Colleagues 73

First Day of Fall — Not the Season, But A Person 74

First Day Someone Complained About My Job 75

First Day Someone Appreciated My Job and Gave Me A Winter Jacket 76

First Paycheck: Not Really Greener Pastures? 77

First Day I Became A Certified Nurse in Canada (Registered Practical Nurse) 78

First Winter—The Season: The Night is Long And Cold 79

First Time Being Discriminated 81

First Time to Quit A Job 83

First Leap of Faith—Going Back to the Operating Room 84

References 87

Acknowledgement 88

About the Author 90

What's next? 91

"When you are inspired by some great purpose, some extraordinary project, all your thoughts break their bounds. Your mind transcends limitations, your consciousness expands in every direction and you find yourself in a new, great and wonderful world. Dormant forces, faculties and talents become alive, and you discover yourself to be a greater person by far than you ever dreamed yourself to be."

Patanjali

Introduction

Have you asked yourself, why does nobody seem interested in the skill set you have for all you know you have been the best in your field? You've submitted your resumes thousand times, and those who call are actually your least desired jobs. You do go to the interviews, but you don't feel good about them.

I had a day like that where after finishing a job interview, I wanted to call all my friends and get drunk. It was so bad because I was caught off guard. I thought I was prepared for the interview, but I realized a health care job interview is a different ball game. Fortunately, I learned from it. I learned the essentials of writing a resume, cover letter, and the techniques needed for a health care job interview.

This knowledge gave me four different major health care jobs, five job offers, and seven various interviews. All in four years. As a newcomer in Canada, landing your dream job in four years is quite an achievement!

These past few years, I realized that everything runs like a business of selling and buying. In a competitive job market, we sell our services to those who are in need of our skill set. Unfortunately, we are in a time when the supply of services is more than the demands. With these new challenges, including being a newcomer, how will you stand out from the competition? How will you get your dream job?

You know what you deserve. You just have to work for it.

Every one of us has a service to offer. Everybody, whether we like it or not. If we want people to pay for our service, we have to sell ourselves. We are now in the business of marketing our skills in the noisy and highly competitive job market.

When you know how to market yourself on your resume, create your elevator pitch through your cover letter, and present your product (yourself) during an interview, you are in control of the game. You can choose which skill set you can highlight and which jobs to apply.

Let me help you transform your resume into an interesting business card. Draft your cover letter into an effective elevator pitch. Transform your awkward style of interviewing into your memorable brand. These are all based on my experience, workshops, and events I have attended, and advice from the incredible people I have met.

Remember, in buying a product, we don't usually buy what we need, we buy what would make us feel good—our wants. After reading this and applying all the techniques, your prospective employer will want you and demand you to work for your dream job! If this all sounds awesome to you, then read on.

Happy job hunting!

Chester Gonzales, foreignurse

PART I
CREATING YOUR BUSINESS CARD

"Did you bring your resume?" my preceptor asked me.

"Yes," I answered.

"Great! Let's meet her."

This was the third day of my consolidation. I went quickly to the changing room, and took out two pieces of paper, secured tidily in a folder: my resume. My preceptor thought I would be a good fit for the operating room nurse position in the Children's Hospital since I had six years of OR experience behind me. I was hopeful.

"We also had a student before who was good. I told her to apply too. I heard she did," my preceptor told me as she unconsciously broke my heart. If there are good candidates applying too, whom the staff knew, what was my edge?

We knocked on the manager's door and as it opened, I sheepishly introduced myself. I handed her my resume, which she accepted with a smile. "Candidates usually apply online," she told me.

I did. I applied online the moment I had the chance. Two more months of night shifts at my other job had passed before I received the call. She wanted to book me for an interview. I passed Level 1.

***

The best thing I did a few months after my arrival in Canada was search for organizations which helped newcomers settle, look for jobs, and enrich themselves. I decided to expand my network, so the chances of succeeding were high. Through Catholic Centre for Immigration and

LASI World Skills, I joined a program called Career Transitions. This was the first free workshop I participated in where they introduced us to the healthcare labor market and the how's of getting the right job for international medical doctors and international health professionals.

We studied resume and cover letter writing and how to ace the interview. All the tips and tricks and my personal experience opened doors of opportunity for me until I finally landed my ideal job.

One thing that I learned from this course was the purpose of the resume.

Resume will not give you "the job." Think of it as a business card that we leave if we want people to contact and do business with us. If the employer calls you for an interview, then the resume has served its purpose. Level one achieved.

Have you ever tried booking a doctor's appointment? When we don't have their number and address saved in our phone, we look for their business card and call them. Why do we need to see a doctor? Because we want to consult with them with regards to our health.

You as the client who needs to see the doctor and calling him is like the employer who needs an employee. Thus, if your resume shows that they can use your skillset to answer their needs, then a call is guaranteed. One of the reasons why you have to focus on acing your resume so that it will stand out from the thousands of applicants: it has to sell you.

A business card tells everything, especially contact numbers, title, and services being offered. Your resume, however, should tell more in a short glimpse of the inattentive personnel who scans resume before it goes to the hiring manager. Two pages max should tell them that you are the one they need.

Ten Tips to Transform your Resume so that it is Interesting for Prospective Employers

1. Use the right resume format: The Combination Resume

Resume style varies. There are chronological, functional, and combination resume styles. Depending on your goal on how you want to sell yourself, you can use any of these to your advantage. What I used and has been recommended to me is the combination resume.

Combination resumes use the key elements of the other two formats. It highlights your qualifications followed by your experiences. An example of a combination resume style is on the next page.

JUAN DELA CRUZ, RN
555 Toronto Road, Ottawa, Ontario, H0H 0H0
(613) 123-4567(c) (613) 891-0000(h) juandelacruz@yahoo.ca

PROFILE

- A competent operating room nurse with eight years of experience, and internationally trained in a 200-bed capacity hospital in the Philippines catering to trauma, geriatric, adult and pediatric surgical cases.
- Completed the OR-RN Course certificate at Foreignurse University and completed consolidation at Major General Hospital Ottawa.
- Two years of nursing home experience and able to identify clients' individual holistic needs and responds therapeutically according to the care plan in a geriatric setting.
- Awarded six times as Most Outstanding Staff Nurse and a recipient of Perfect Attendance Commendation annually for seven years.
- Awarded with Best in Clinical Practice and Best in Academic Performance in the collegiate years.

Languages: English and Filipino
Computer Skills: Microsoft Word, PowerPoint, Excel, Publisher, Email, and Internet Searching

EXPERIENCE

Canadian
Registered Nurse　　　　　　　　　　　　　　　　　　　　　　　　　May 1, 2015 – Present
ForeigNursing Home
420 Toronto Road, Ottawa, Ontario H0H 0H0

- Develops and implements nursing care plan.
- Assesses residents' health status and identifies abnormal changes and intervenes.
- Administers medication (oral, subcutaneous, intramuscular), which includes narcotics, assuming responsibility for possession of keys.
- Mentors new staff in proper care and techniques in relation to caring for residents according to care plan.
- Carries out doctor's orders and communicates to pharmacy, laboratory, and CCAC if necessary.

Personal Support Worker - Unregulated Care Provider　　　　　　August 5, 2014 – April 30, 2014
ForeigNursing Retirement Residence
840 Toronto Road, Ottawa, Ontario, H0H 0H0

- Teamed up with other nursing staff and team members in aiding the residents in their medications and their activity of daily living.
- Provided support to residents in meeting their daily needs while maintaining their independence.
- Gave baths, rendered morning and evening care, and helped residents during meals.

International
Operating Room—Recovery Room Staff Nurse March 2, 2006—May 15, 2014
PinoyNurse Medical Center
Cabanatuan City, Nueva Ecija, Philippines, 3100

- Performed individualized plan of care for patients who underwent various surgical intervention.
- Assigned as a charge nurse who managed and led the unit, mentored, and coached new staff nurse.
- Collaborated with the surgical team with efficiency in a circulator and scrub role, thus ensuring patient safety.
- Involved in writing of the annual revision of unit's policy for continuous quality improvement.

Operating Room Clinical Instructor (Part time) March 2009—February 2014

PinoyNurse University
Cabanatuan City, Nueva Ecija, Philippines

- Presented theory to students and clarified concepts that were misunderstood.
- Assisted students in actual performance of operating room procedures and care and gave feedback to develop the skills which need improvement.
- Evaluated students through written and practical examination and made sure topics were understood.
- Utilized necessary techniques to facilitate learning and understanding for the students in order to give appropriate care to patients.

Editor in Chief—"Foreignurse" 2009-2012
PinoyNurse Medical Center
Cabanatuan City, Nueva Ecija, Philippines, 3100

- Lead the creation of the first official nursing (English) publication in the province, which gives information about updates in the institution as well as provides entertainment to readers.
- Completed publication under a tight schedule.
- Conducted workshops for new writers and members for the publication.

EDUCATION

Continuing Education

Registered Nurse—Operating Room Certificate Program August - December 2017
Foreignurse University
1723 Toronto Road
Ottawa, Ontario H0H H0H

Master of Arts in Nursing 2007-2009
Pilipino University
Cabanatuan City, Nueva Ecija, Philippines, 3100

Nursing Education

Bachelor of Science in Nursing

2. Know the anatomy of a combination resume and supply it with relevant and significant information.

Anatomy of Combination Resume

a. The Header

b. Profile

c. Experience

d. Education

e. Other relevant data

---

a) The Header

JUAN DELA CRUZ, RN
555 Toronto Road, Ottawa, Ontario, H0H0H0
(613) 123-4567(c) (613) 891-0000(h) juandelacruz@yahoo.ca

- This is where you put your name and contact information. I recommend placing it in the center although you can put it as left-justified. Make sure your name is all in capital letters and in bold font.

- Some recommend that you don't have to put your title (RN, RPN/LPN, NP) after your name. Although some jobs specify which nurses they need, others do not. For those employers who want either an RN or an RPN, I recommend putting your title, so your employer doesn't have to guess. If, of course, you are applying to a field other than nursing, then your title is irrelevant.

    - Important to note that nursing titles are legally bound. Put RN or RPN/LPN only if you are a certified nurse in the country where you are working (e.g., Canada). Do not put RN because you are an RN in the Philippines but not in Canada, and you are applying to a Canadian workplace.

- Always write your complete address and do not use abbreviations.
- Put contact numbers where you can be reached, and where they can leave a message for you. I usually put my cellphone and home phone number as my contact numbers, but I put my cellphone number first to imply that I prefer to be called on my cellphone first. As above I put (c) to indicate a cell number and (h) to indicate home. If you don't have a house number or if a message can't be left on it (or a cellphone) then just put the number to which they can reach you.
- Do not forget to put your email address. Make sure it is easy to spell and remember. If you have to create a new one for this purpose, do so (as long as you check it regularly). It is not recommended to have email addresses where the names are spelled backward (tnecniv.retsehc@yahoo.ca), or with weird numeric combinations (chester32658@hotmail.com), or bizarre and informal phrases (cute_and_handsome_CallMe@forPete'sSake.com).

b) Profile

Profiles on your resume are critical as they are the first description the employer will read about you. It is recommended to have a series of short statements on five points. Never sell yourself short on this. If you are highly skilled, don't put skillful. Use powerful words as your keywords.

When I applied as a personal support worker and practical nursing jobs in homes, the first point in my profile is this:

- A competent caregiver who identifies a client's individual holistic needs and responds therapeutically according to the plan of care.

    Using strong keywords like "competent" creates good impression. There is a high chance that they will read through the whole resume.

When I applied as an operating room nurse, I highlighted my operating room nursing experience.

- A well-skilled operating room nurse with six years of experience and internationally trained in a Level IV hospital in the Philippines doing both scrub and circulating roles.

Do not forget to never short sell yourself by not adding any strong and relevant adjectives. If I put 'An OR nurse with six years of experience...' it wouldn't differ from those who applied with five, ten, or twelve years of experience. A strong adjective will set you apart from others.

When I attended a job fair as part of a youth leadership workshop, there were no healthcare facilities participating in the fair. We were told that the employers would include those from other industries like clothing and food services. This reminds me of some newcomers who apply for survival jobs other than the healthcare industry. For this, I changed the first point on my resume and submitted my resume to a clothing line I thought I might consider joining.

- Awarded three times as Most Outstanding Staff and a recipient of Perfect Attendance Commendation annually for six years.

Make sure your first point will lead your prospective employer to read the other four points and the whole resume. Don't forget to paint a picture on your statement. "Level IV hospital" has more impact than "one of the hospitals"; "Awarded three times" and "annually for six years" is better than a "recipient of numerous awards."

Remember to keep it short. A maximum of two- or three-line sentences is better. Bear in mind that your resume will be skimmed and should spark interest.

PROFILE

- A competent operating room nurse with eight years of experience, and internationally trained in a 200-bed capacity hospital in the Philippines catering trauma, geriatric, adult and pediatric surgical cases.
- Completed the OR-RN Course certificate at Foreignurse University and completed consolidation at Major General Hospital Ottawa.
- With two years of nursing home experience who identifies client's individual holistic needs and responds therapeutically according to the care plan in a geriatric setting.
- Have awarded six times as Most Outstanding Staff Nurse and a recipient of Perfect Attendance Commendation annually for seven years.
- Awarded with Best in Clinical Practice and Best in Academic Performance in the collegiate years.

Languages: English and Filipino
Computer Skills: Microsoft Word, PowerPoint, Excel, Publisher, Email, and Internet Searching

The first statement may highlight your years of experience if that is one of your assets, and it is relevant to the job post. For example, years of nursing experience if in nursing field, or years of caregiving or customer service experience, whichever is pertinent to the job. Don't forget to specify the number of years and place a strong adjective before it.

Furthermore, the second statement highlights the other important qualifications based on the job requirements. Are they looking for a specific course certificate? Are they looking for someone who has experience in medication administration? Showcase your relevant expertise in this part.

The rest of your statements must present other skills or assets which are relevant to the qualifications needed by the employer.

c) **Experience**

- As shown in the example above, we can write the following here:
    - Job Title opposite the dates of employment
    - Name of employer
    - Employer's location including the country
    - Job description

d) Education

- This is usually placed at the bottom of a combination resume. It is significant, especially if the job requires a special certificate like in the above example where the (assumed) job (posting) requires finishing an OR course.

- Also, this should be presented with the dates when the course was completed or enrolled opposite the program, the university or college where it was taken, and the address and country of the school attended.

e) Other relevant data

Languages: English and Filipino
Computer Skills: Microsoft Word, PowerPoint, Excel, Publisher, Email, and Internet Searching

3. How to present your work experience: highlight your skill set from your past employers

Resumes must tell one story: your qualifications that tempt the employer to call you and discuss more about you. It should spark interest.

If you succeeded in grabbing the attention of the hiring manager throughout your profile and impressing them, she will now take notes on where you have worked and what skills have you applied or mastered in your past workplace.

Your work experience comes second on your combination resume. As an internationally educated professional, I categorized my work experience into two: Canadian and International. If you don't have Canadian work experience but have volunteer experience in Canada, you can include that on your resume. If you don't have any Canadian experience at all, then you can put your international experience.

It is recommended that you put job descriptions with at least three one or two line bulleted statements below your job title. Use action words or verbs at the beginning of each sentence.

The tricky part of constructing the statements here is the usage of the tenses of verbs. Use past tense when you describe your job description from your previous job, but for present employers, use verbs to describe your job description in the present tense.

Collectively, the employer must see the skill sets you have applied and mastered on your present and past jobs. If you wrote administered medication, as one of your job descriptions on your past job, do not put the same description over and over if you have the same role in your other past jobs unless you are applying as a medication nurse (hence highlight this skill—but make sure you write the statements differently). Instead, show other skills you have gained from the other previous jobs like how you mentored newly hire staff

I worked in three homes before I got my operating room nurse job. I had the same role in these homes. What I did since I stayed at my first job for three years, and with casual status to other two, I highlighted my first job by giving more details to my job description, and on some of my resumes, I did not put my other two. The reason for this is because I want to limit my resume to two sheets and to avoid redundancy of job description that would waste the prospective employer's time. Also, my first job shows that I don't have an employment gap since I started working in Canada. Lastly, I want to highlight my international OR experience that if I included my other jobs, the resume would be too long to even be considered by an employer. Remember, keep it short and significant.

Do not forget to modify your job description according to the skills they require on the job posting.

If you worked in fast food before (survival job) and want to apply to a healthcare job, you can include the skills you gained and used such as how you took care your customers, led your team, and reminded your staff to maintain cleanliness on your job description. The examples below are job description statements if you want to use your fast food crew experience for applying to the healthcare industry (verbs are in the past tense, as if it is your past job. If it is your current job, then make it present tense):

- Provided satisfaction to customer by meeting their needs and addressing their wants throughout the entire experience.
- Ensured the cleanliness of the facility and emphasized the health effects of an unclean environment to my team.
- Led the team to be more productive by motivating them to do their best every time.

Furthermore, if you are from a healthcare industry and want to apply to other industries, you can use your transferable skills on your resumes. Remember that all industries required creative, helping, management, leadership, technical, and organizational skills. Find out how you have utilized these skills to work and show it on your resume. When I applied for a clothing store, I emphasized on my resume my customer service skills since nursing is customer service itself. I was called for an interview but needed to cancel it since I was not interested in the job anymore.

4. Tailor your resume according to the employer's needs

Having a master resume at hand is great. However, having the same resume that you use in applying for different jobs is a guaranteed fail.

I have a master resume on my computer. During the Career Transition course, we were asked to create one master resume. This resume, however, is not a print and send, or download and send, document to every job opening. It served as my go-to-edit format if needed. I probably have more than ten of my resume samples being revised and updated on my desktop. Reading my profile highlights above, you might have guessed that I tailored my resume depending on the needs of the employer.

This brings us the importance of reading the job opening qualifications. How can your resume answer the call for the job? Are they looking for someone who has at least two years of experience? If so, then highlight in your profile your years of experience (given that you have at least two). Do they want a special certificate course? Then highlight that you have completed the course and with honors. Do they want someone with a good record of professionalism? Then write about your outstanding record of no late and absences.

I hope you know what I mean. If the employer is looking for bananas, give them bananas. Of course, given that you have bananas to offer. Some of the job openings here in Ottawa required bilingual (English and French) applicants. I am bilingual but not French, so I didn't apply to those openings. But if the job specifies that being bilingual applicant is "preferred" rather than "required," then I try my luck—which happened with my current job. I got lucky.

5. Finding the right job ads for you

How do you know that you are a good fit for the job?

You are the best candidate for the job, you don't have to tell me. And so are the hundreds or thousands of applicants who submitted their resume. Why do they need Canadian credentials if you have your whole working years of experience behind you from your home country? Is being a bookworm an advantage if I wanted to be a bookstore employee? I can recommend books to customers, that should be it, right?

No. It's not. It is recommended that you meet at least 60% of the requirement to be seriously considered. If you do look for some job ads, be mindful between the essential and the desirable requirements.

The following is an example of a job ad I have found online (ca.indeed.com). If you've noticed, they are looking for either RN or LPN as a good candidate.

Highlighted in red are the "essential" requirements. Take note of the word "required," "must have," "must be," etc. Moreover, highlighted in yellow are the "desirable" qualifications.

As can be seen on the posting, they are looking for an Alberta registered nurse (RN or LPN) who must have a strong clinical background. If you read further, they need someone with 1-2 years of clinical experience. With these cues, you can highlight on your profile your years of clinical experience (even international experience) and expertise in dealing with pediatric clients; knowledge of allergy, immunology, asthma, and lactation.

However, allergy, immunology, and asthma experience are "not required." Since the ad states that it is "a plus" but they are willing to train, you can apply to this posting even if you do not have the specific experience. However, you can put it in your cover letter if not in the resume that you are willing to train or are a highly trainable individual.

Registered Nurse - RN/LPN position
Smile Buddy - Calgary, AB
$40 - $50 an hour - Full-time, Part-time

We are currently seeking a motivated and organized RN or LPN to join our *pediatric Allergy and lactation consultation clinic* in the SW community of Seton. This is an excellent opportunity to work at a new practice and make a gratifying career out of it. You must have a strong clinical background and enjoy pediatric patient contact. Leadership ability is a must. We are seeking an individual with excellent interpersonal communication skills, strong problem solving skills and the ability to prioritize and multitask under pressure.

Job Duties Include:
- Allergy testing and pulmonary function testing
- Extract preparation
- Food oral challenge
- Administer subcutaneous allergy shots
- Patient Calls
- Provides skilled lactation care and instruction to breastfeeding mothers and infants
- Organize and assist in the development, implementation and evaluation of policies, procedures and patient/staff education materials.

Work Week:
- Full time – Four days – 37 Hr.
- Work Week — No weekends or holidays.

Qualifications:
- Must be an RN/LPN licensed in Alberta
- Allergy, Asthma & Immunology experience would be a plus but will train the right candidate
- BLS Certified
- Requires basic Computer skills
- Ability to work independently with good nursing judgment, self-motivation and self-confidence
- Be able to recognize and manage anaphylaxis

Required education:
Hospital Certification program, Associates Degree or better
Required experience: Clinical: 1 — 2 years

Job Type: Full-time

Please email me back your resume if you're interested in knowing more information and we could schedule an interview.
Have a wonderful day,
Mostafa
Job Types: Full-time, Part-time

6. Using Keywords to fit your resume to the job posting.

Tip 4 emphasizes the importance of tailoring your resume. Tip 5 meanwhile taught you how to spot a job ad that fits for you. This next tip combines the two through using keywords.

Furthermore, Tip 4 tells you to give them bananas if they want bananas—given that you have bananas. Now, how will you show your prospective employer that you have bananas, and yours are the best ones?

Using keywords will make your resume stand out. Some employers have scanning programs that scan the words between your resume and the job posting. The more "hits" the machine recognize, the more promising your resume is. Keywords are phrases that you incorporate to your resume that are based on the job ads that you are applying to.

By considering the qualifications they are seeking from the job ads posted above, the whole resume should respond to their needs. You can observe below the examples of how the use of almost the same words between the ads and resume (highlighted) are utilized as the keywords.

- A proficient registered nurse with four years of <u>clinical experience</u> in a 200-bed capacity <u>hospital</u>... *(part of your profile)*
- Appointed as the team <u>leader</u> of the unit... *(part of one of your job descriptions in the experience part)*
- Improved <u>policies</u> of the unit... *(part of one of your job descriptions in the experience part)*
- <u>Computer Skills</u>: Microsoft Word, Excel, Publisher... *(added on the other relevant data)*

7. Get to know your transferrable skills

Transferable skills are the "common denominator" skills that underlie all job functions according to the workbook we used in the Career Transition program for IMDs. It also stated that employment experts agree that skill identification is essential to a successful job search. It refers to your abilities or what you can do for your prospects that you should identify to compete in the market. How much do you know yourself? What are your selling points?

The nursing field requires specialized knowledge that not all people can do unless they undergo the program or course. However, nursing practice entails a collaborative set of skills other than the knowledge we acquired from our universities and colleges.

We should not forget that nurses have a myriad of roles. We are caregivers, educators, technicians, advocates, leaders, managers, advisors and many more. Furthermore, as individuals, we acquire skills outside of nursing. Some of us are writers, poets, singers, musicians, entrepreneurs, and artists.

When we came to Canada and started from zero, we had the choice to pursue our profession or make a transition. Career changes are common. Whatever would make us happy is an important element of living. If you decide to do jobs other than nursing or perhaps start a survival job, always look into what you can do for your future bosses. Bosses vary from the conventional to the public or to yourself.

During the course, I remembered that we took the whole three hours or so to discuss this. The most important element of identifying your transferable skills is to get to know yourself in depth. Then knowing what you want to do and the skills that you want to exhibit. This is helpful when you are creating your profile and job description.

If you decide to become an insurance agent, you can emphasize all the skills that you have right now to the skills required as an agent. The likes of having superb communication skills, leadership and management skills are a sure advantage in the position. How about applying as a manager or supervisor of a store? What transferrable skills do you have that you can showcase on your resume and interviews that would impress your prospective employer?

8. Managing electronic resume

When I arrived in Canada and started applying for jobs, I realized that the majority of job postings are online. I had to send many resume online—which I am not used to. What I was used to was submitting my two pieces of paper directly to the hiring manager. Although most of the jobs I have been hired for were through my network and sending my resume offline, I applied to my present job both online and offline.

I remember when I was browsing around on job sites and just sent my resume in. For two months I didn't receive any calls. I also tried going around malls and shopping plazas to see which stores were hiring and grab some applications to fill out. Nobody called probably because my resume wasn't flexible then.

Fast forward to when I learned resume writing and posted it online and competed on the market, 90% of job applications I have applied for and other opportunities (volunteering) have called me. Until now, I am still receiving job offers online. It may be luck, but in a competitive world, I wouldn't risk a slim chance.

Browsing the net to get some tips on how to format and send a resume electronically, I came across this site (https://www.sovren.com/faq/TipsForElectronicResumes.pdf), which has a PDF guide for e-resume formatting. Sovren Group (according to the site) has over 20 years of experience in providing software to automatically understand and classify all data contained within resumes. From their description, we know that "really" there is a software which scans our resume submitted online before some human contact.

Below are some tips taken from the site. I recommend you review the whole guide.

- Always use a Microsoft Word format.
  - I am a fan of PDF myself, but according to the website, employers prefer an editable resume being submitted to them. Being able to edit it on their side may be an advantage to your resume.
- A plain resume is better than a fancy looking one for computer scanners.
  - This means don't put anything in the header and footer. Do not use tables or other graphics (pictures, Word Art, etc.) on your resume. Do not put page numbers, either. Only capitalize what is necessary like the letters of your name and the category title (PROFILE). One reference suggested the use of typefaces fonts like Arial and Verdana.
- Do not use resume templates, especially if it suggests putting tables.
- NEVER omit dates on work history. Formatted as month and year (March 2008—Present) is recommended.
- Do not include references on your resume. References are asked during the interview, and it is disrespectful to display your references' contact numbers to different job sites where you are applying.

9. Character references

Before I left the Philippines, I requested two recommendation letters from both my head nurse and the chief nurse. I would recommend you do the same thing since as a newcomer, it would be a challenge to gather a work-related reference whom your prospective employer can contact without effort (since you haven't work yet—I assume).

Moreover, I would also suggest you join workshops and courses which aim to help you professionally. Through these gatherings you will meet others and grow a network which you can use as an academic reference (facilitators of the course/organizers/ trainers).

Furthermore, once you have gained employment, always be the best employee. Treat your colleagues well and maintain a good relationship with your manager. Remember that these colleagues will be your future references if you need to apply to more jobs.

My former manager hated me for leaving her team of nurses. But she's the one who encouraged me to grab the opportunities ahead of me. Up until now, we have a good relationship, and I know that if need be, she'll be more than willing to give me a very good reference. Not to mention my other nurse colleagues who became my references, which gave me other part-time jobs. Also, my former head nurse in the Philippines has been my friend until now.

Additionally, I remember when I applied for a volunteer position, they needed four references. The institution where I applied for printed out questionnaires for them. What I did since I don't have any work-related reference during that time, I have asked my friends back home to ask my head nurse and supervisors to fill it out and scan back the forms to me. I then printed out the completed forms, and the institution accepted these.

Lastly, don't hesitate to give an international reference. On my present job, I must give two managers as references. One manager from my former employer and my Filipino OR head nurse. Nowadays, there are many ways for your employer to contact your reference. One method is through questionnaires sent via email.

When an employer asks for your references, it means that they are interested in hiring you. Do not include your references in your resume. Do not put "reference upon request" on it since it doesn't tell anything. Also, do not attach your references with your resume unless otherwise requested by the employer. More importantly, always inform your references that you will provide their contact information and they might receive a call and/or an email.

10. Final Touches

Incorrect spelling and poor grammar throughout your resume are a major turn off to prospective employers. Remember that your potential employer has only 15 seconds to scan your resume. Often, they have scan system that filters the qualified from non-qualified, and this is based on the keywords your resume has provided (for example: "required: experienced nurse; keyword: with six years of experience as a nurse").

Please set aside the time to proofread your resume. It is helpful to have another person look it over (and preferably an English speaker). Also, you can use apps like Grammarly to check your work. Moreover, what I usually do, in my articles and the same with my resumes, I let it sit for a day or two then reread it. It will give me time to review my work with a different mindset. If it sounds wrong, it is probably wrong. If it sounds redundant, it probably is.

Make sure it is readable and appealing to the eyes. Fonts must be in between 10-14. Do not overload information on your resume then adjusting fonts to smaller just to fit into two pages. Remove irrelevant information or the least important and highlight the most important. Have plenty of white space. Margins are 1.25 cm at the top and bottom and 2.25cm along both sides.

Always remember that your resume has to sell you a spot for an interview. Look at your resume. Scan it. Read it. Do you like the person written in your resume? Are you impressed by the skills described in it? Is it tailored to the job opening? Will the employer be interested in meeting you?

If you feel good about it, then be ready to suit up. Claim the completion of level one.

When God gave me the opportunity to go back to work in the operating room, I gave my 100% in constructing my resume and giving my all to the interview. I have proven one thing from this experience which I wish to remind everybody: If you really want something to happen, give your 100% to achieve it. Remember that extraordinary things are the result of extraordinary action.

PART II

ELEVATING YOUR ELEVATOR PITCH

Ding.

Elevator door opens.

My manager came in, "Hi. How are you?" she asked me.

"I'm good, and yourself?" I asked back.

"Good."

I nodded my head and smiled.

Then there was an awkward silence.

Ding.

The elevator door opens. I walked out.

I felt that I could have done better.

I have learned the concept of elevator pitch through the "Launch" program, a free course for youths who want to start a business. In the program, they wanted us to conceptualize or create a business, and in 15 seconds (just like in an elevator ride), we should present the business concept to a prospective customer.

This is like the ads we watch every day. An average commercial usually only lasts about 15-30 seconds since it is expensive to show a TV ad and it costs every second. The creative and marketing department of a company must convey their message to this limited time frame. They must be creative to catch the attention of their audience. The challenge also is how will the product or the service be memorable to the market.

My elevator encounter with my manager happened when I am already her staff. That's a good thing because I have done better on other days, meaning less awkward moment. But your job application doesn't always have some other days.

What helps your resume show the more of you? What is the elevator pitch of your job application? Your cover letter is your elevator pitch. Your supplemental commercial. It has to convey your message, and it has to adhere to your prospective employer.

Once you've submitted your resume, without the cover letter, it will not convey "more" of you. But writing it the wrong way, it takes away the opportunity to capture the attention of the employer to get in touch with you.

You have to remember that the employer has a very short amount of time. Introducing yourself, the position you want to apply to, and where you'd find out the job posting is a waste of both of your time.

So please do not include the following in your cover letter:

> Good day.
>
> I am Juan Dela Cruz, and I am applying for the position of staff nurse in your company. I have seen a job posting online and I am interested to be a part of your prestigious institution. Blah blah blah blah

This is a complete waste of time of the reader/ prospective employer. First, your name is indicated in the header. Second, the company is aware they have posted vacancies online. Lastly, they don't need to know that you are interested in applying for the position since it is obvious.

Three Tips for Effective Cover Letter Writing

1. Make every part of the cover letter counts.

Cover letters are like an elevator pitch that must catch the employer's attention given the short period of time the reader has. It must stick in the short glimpse. Each part of it should not waste the reader's time and should tell more about yourself. This should sell so they will be curious to read your resume. That's how they should feel.

- Put the same header as your resume. Follow the same guidelines in writing the header.

- Don't forget to put the current date of the application. Following this includes the address of the company. If you know the manager or the hiring manager, put their name, title, and designation.

- In the salutation part, it would be impressive to address the right person. If you can research whom to address the letter through phone call or website, it would be remarkable. Although, sometimes it is not possible to get the hiring manager's name. In this instance, they recommend the use of "Dear Hiring Manager."

- The subject line includes the position you are applying to. Remember that some job postings have a competition number or specific assigned name. Put this as the subject line for clarity, especially since so many resumes are coming in applying to different positions. The subject line is written like the example below.

- The body of the letter usually comprises of 3-4 paragraphs. Workitdaily.com describes these four paragraphs as follow: The Grab, The Hook, The Paragraph of Knowledge and the Close.

- The Grab—"I saw your posting online, and I am interested in being part of your institution" is not a grabber opening paragraph. It doesn't tell anything about you. The first sentence and/or your paragraph should highlight why you are the best candidate for the job. Grab their attention. Impress them.

- The Hook—Once you have grabbed the attention of the hiring manager, you have to hook them with more of your credential highlights. You can bullet your qualifications as a list. You can also emphasize here how your experience qualifies you for the job posted.

Chester Gonzales

JUAN DELA CRUZ, RN ← Header
555 Toronto Road, Ottawa, Ontario, H0H0H0
(613) 123-4567(c) (613) 891-0000(h) juandelacruz@yahoo.ca

April 5, 2018 ← Current Date

Mr. Ronald McDonald, BScN, RN
Manager, Perioperative Services
Major General Hospital ← The address of the company you're
800 Toronto Road, applying and the name and the title of
Ottawa, Ontario H0H H0H the person you're addressing

Dear Mr. McDonald: ← The Salutation

RE: Operating Room Registered Nurse Competition Number 5678 ← Subject line

With my extensive experience as a perioperative nurse in the Philippines and my completed OR-RN certificate course at Foreignurse University and consolidation at Major General Hospital, my background, skills, and knowledge will greatly be useful in joining your competent team of perioperative nurses.

Throughout the eight years of perioperative nursing, I have played different roles in the OR team. I have practiced my circulating and scrub roles to various cases with different complexities. Most importantly, as a perioperative nurse, I have understood the significance of maintaining the safety of the patient by proper handling of instruments, maintaining of the sterile field, vigilance in the sponge count, participating in the surgical pause and being the patient's advocate.

My dedication to perioperative nursing reflects my decision to enroll myself to OR-RN course and be able to embrace once again the challenges of the Operating Room. I have completed my consolidation at MGH and been commended by many OR personnel. My preceptor evaluated my clinical competency as "extremely competent", excellent in professionalism and asserted that I will be a great asset to any operating room.

I look forward to discussing with you in details the ways in which I can bring significant value to MGH as one of your staff, and I invite you to contact me at your convenience.

Yours truly,

Juan Dela Cruz, RN

Grab Hook, Knowledge, Close — Body of letter: 3-4 paragraphs

- The Paragraph of Knowledge—this part will either showcase how knowledgeable you are in the position you are applying or to the company that you have applied for. In the example given, it shows how Juan Del Cruz pursues his OR passion plus how he was commended while working with the staff at the MGH. However, if the example doesn't apply to you, then you can do research about the company, its mission, and its vision. Through this research, you can incorporate how your skills can contribute to achieving the company's mission.

- Close - Your final paragraph should wrap up the whole letter. Here you can suggest a meeting or ask them to contact you at their most convenient time.

- Do not forget about your complimentary close. I usually use "Yours truly," with a comma at the end. You can also use "Sincerely." Two-line space apart is your signature line. I suggest putting your title (RN/RPN) after your name, separated by a comma. Use ink if possible, in signing the line.

2. Your cover letter is not a paragraph form of your resume.

It is tempting to write a narrative of your resume in the cover letter. After all, what is written in your resume are the highlights of your qualifications and career. But don't make this mistake. Do not regurgitate information from your resume. If you do this then you lose the opportunity to sell more of yourself. As much as possible, new informational highlights and selling points are what should be written in your cover letter.

Moreover, if two pages are recommended for a resume, the cover letter should only have one page. Make it brief. Remember the concept of an elevator pitch. It must be short but catches attention and shows more of you. Every point of your cover letter must link to the position's requirements and your background.

3. Customize your cover letter according to the position you are applying and your prospective employer.

Just like your resume, your cover letter must be tailored according to the position you are applying and the employer you are sending. Remember the parts of your resume. Your qualification highlights must compensate for the qualifications the employer is seeking. Also, your paragraph of knowledge must reflect how much you know about the institution.

If they are looking for someone with superb leadership and communication skills, you can write about these skills of yours in the letter. If they want someone who has finished a certificate, you can highlight that you acquired one and with impressive grades.

Also, it would be impressive on the part of the employer if through your letter it shows how much research you went through to know the company. Maybe you can write about how their philosophy as an institution has the same values as yours at work. How about how your skill set can help them in the future expansion of the company?

Part III
Building Your Brand: Intervene in Interview Disasters

If resumes give them access to what you offer, then the cover letter tells them more about you. During your interview, you show them what you've got and what you're made of. You build your brand.

Think of the interview as unboxing a product. You are the product. The interview event is how they are going to unbox you. Will they like what they see? They should or else they will ship you back to either unemployment, your crappy job, or your low-paying job.

The challenge here is how they would love the product once they unbox? Moreover, there are at least three products to unbox, how do you make sure that you won't be the one to be shipped back? The solution: you must be irresistible. You must be the iPhone they are looking for amidst all the androids. You must be the Coca-Cola among all the sugar water. You must build a brand that sticks.

***

"Yes, Mr. Customer Service with a big smile, you're hired!"

There was excitement in the room as he handed me the paper where I found my interview results, which were marked "hired." Among the fifteen participants, I am one of the three hired.

It was a mock interview at one of the workshops I attended. We were given the task to look for a real job posting, then during our final week, we would be interviewed based on the posting we submitted to.

I found an online posting for a medical secretary at one of the clinics in Ottawa. Back then, I was still an uncertified nurse who wanted to apply in a healthcare-related job. Through this workshop, I witnessed how some applicants fail during interviews. We were given a few days of lectures on how to act during an interview, but many forgot the most important guidelines. Also, during this mock interview, you could feel the pressure as we were being interviewed by intimidating personnel (more than one), video recorded, and watched by our co-participants. Suffice to say, the pressure is real.

From that experience a few years ago, and from the experience of a few rejected interviews, I will list the disasters that I have done and observed from others so that you can avoid having your own interview disasters. I have categorized these disasters into three and provided different examples for each. Later, we will be focusing more on the know-how of an interview session and the appropriate remedies to the following disaster below.

Three Most Common Disasters During Interview

1. Failure To Research And Ignoring Small Details Disasters

- You don't know what you put in your resume and cover letter.

- You don't know the job you are applying to or the required qualifications. I have seen some of my colleagues who applied to certain jobs and not even bother to research the acronyms listed in the job posting. Hence, during the interview, they have no idea when asked about those. Clearly, they don't qualify.

- You don't like what you are applying to. Why did you even apply? Is it just because you needed a job? Save yourself some time and misery. Do not do this, please. Find something that would worth your time and your resources. You might pass the interview process, but you don't want to be miserable every day.

- You don't like yourself. This is trouble. For you to be able to sell yourself, you must believe in the skill set that you are selling. I know people struggle, and we sometimes have problems with self-esteem. But during the interview process, you must like yourself, so the interviewer will like you. If you are having an inner struggle with yourself, and you can fake during the interview moment, that is fine, as long as it can help you get the job. We don't know, the job might be able to help you feel esteemed. However, if this is an ongoing battle within yourself and you're having trouble uplifting yourself, seek help. Keep in touch with friends who remind you of your worth. Talk about this with your family. Seek professional help if need be.

- You didn't sleep well last night, and you have a bad morning. Suffice to say, this won't end up well unless you've practiced meditation or mindfulness hours before the interview. Setting the mind and the mood right will help you a lot in the boiling room. If you really like the job you are applying to, and you know how critical the day of the interview is, make the days before that stress-free. I know things can be out of control, but worst-case scenario, if things get worse the day itself, or the day before, a disaster happened—call the interviewer to reset the schedule. But for some other reasons like you slept in because you got drunk; and your girlfriend got mad at you the day before the interview… Oh come on. You're better than that. Don't mess around with your girlfriend the day before your interview.

- You forgot your interview schedule.

- You are underdressed. Business attire and/or a three-piece suit is not overdressed. Remember the workplace culture. In Canada, it is customary to wear formal business attire to an interview. It shows respect and importance to the interview and to the interviewer. You might feel uncomfortable about wearing this, but you have to try to feel comfortable. Remember that making a good impression is important.

- You bring so much stuff (umbrella, backpack, purse, coat) into the interview room, the interviewer has to think about where you can put your things.

- You are so nervous, and nobody is comfortable in the room. You leave the interviewer wondering if you're okay.

2. Communication Disasters

- You struggle to communicate, and it displeases you.

    As a foreignurse, or someone whose English is a second language in an English setting interview environment, it is natural for us to stutter at times or look for the right words in the English dictionary we store in our brains. Both you and the interviewer know about this. Communication skills are important. These involve both verbal and non-verbal cues. This skill can be developed or practiced. This will be discussed later.

But given your background, always remember that the interviewer will give you time to gather your thoughts and respond accordingly. This applies to other applicants whose English is their first language. They will give time, and they will understand.

However, the more concerning scene here is if it displeases you. You struggle, and stutter and you lose your words, and it bothers you too much. You may be surviving the speaking parts but not the non-verbal part, which is evident on your face. You are grimacing, scratching your head, pounding your forehead, and other unnecessary acts.

3. Interview Q&A Disasters

- You answer the question based on answers found on the internet. Most of the answers found on the internet have been heard many times before by the interviewers. If 9/10 of the participants have answered the same way as they have read on the internet, then the one who has a different answer will be the only person worth remembering. Why is that? Probably because those nine others are forgettable interviews—well, forgettable answers—technically.

- You answer the question with a story that is too long, and everybody, including you, is lost in it. Stories are good for answering interview questions, but if you come unprepared, you may tell a story that is too long or convoluted, leaving you to get lost. Your story may become confusing for many reasons. You are trying to fix your grammar as you talk. Also, you are trying to remember what to say. Then you like to keep your interviewer interested. Using a story will fail if you do not know how to share your story in a short and significant way.

How to tell your story will be discussed later.

- Your story is too personal. Sure, it is hard to gather up stories that you can use to answer questions that will make you stand out. However, a lack of preparation can result in you unloading all your family affairs on the interview table. If you are comfortable sharing your personal stories, the interviewer might get a negative view of you. Remember that they are assessing your work ethic and experience. What they expect you to share is your work experience — not your personal trials and tribulations. Yes, I have witnessed this happened.

- You answer questions based on "what you think you should do as a nurse" and not "what you think you should do if you are hired for the position posted."

This was one of my mistakes and done twice. First was when I applied for a volunteer position as an aid for clients with cancer. I was interviewed by a panel of four people. I actually felt good about the interview, until I received the email that I wasn't fit for the volunteer job.

One of the panels was the facilitator of the workshops I had attended. I met her again for career advice and then she gave me feedback on the interview that she witnessed. I was right, the interview went well, but I answered their questions incorrectly. I answered their questions based on my role as a nurse and not an aid. That was the determining factor since the panel is afraid that I might overdo my job in the sense that I would behave in a way that was out of the line. I thought I understood until a second rejected interview.

I had an interview as a floor nurse in one of the hospitals in Ottawa, and I failed it because I answered the question from an OR nurse perspective and not a floor nurse. More on this in a later discussion.

We should be sure to review the job description and responsibilities in job ads. This will be the basis of the things that you should be doing and probably the basis of the interview question. If for example, you applied for a practical nursing position and you were a registered nurse in your home country, then there are certain responsibilities that RPN cannot do. Limit your answer from the scope of practice you are able to do in the job setting to which you are applying.

- You don't ask questions for clarification. Do not answer any questions that you do not understand. Seek for clarification. You can say things like "Can you repeat that?" or rephrase the question, "Do you mean like…?" You'll be surprised by how the interviewer will actually help you to answer the question.

- You don't ask a question at the end.

    Interviewer: Do you have any question for us?

    You: None. Thanks.

    Okay. You don't seem to be interested in anything related to your prospective employer, the company, or the position.

Five Essential Things to Remember to Avoid Interview Disasters

1. Familiarize yourself with the phases of an interview.

An interview in general has three phases: the introduction, the body of the interview, and the closing part.

Each part is critical for you, and knowing what to do in each phase is significant.

Introduction starts as soon as you step foot in the building. *You have to look pleasant and approachable to every person you are meeting there.* Remember, you don't know who is involved in the interview or who could influence the hiring process. We always see in movies how the candidate disrespects someone who eventually turns out to be the interviewer himself. It happens. Don't make this mistake.

You have to arrive fifteen minutes before your interview schedule. More than fifteen minutes before your scheduled time will make an impression of you having nothing else to do. Also, a wait time of more than fifteen minutes will make you wait for more. How much patience did you bring with you?

Moreover, less than fifteen minutes is okay, as long as you can calm your nerves before your scheduled interview, and you know for sure which room to go to or which person to meet. Being late of course is unacceptable.

Some interview places have reception personnel. *Greet them and make yourself comfortable around them.* They are a big help in case you wanted to ask if you are heading in the right room. Also, if you have lots of luggage behind you, like a coat or umbrella, you can ask them if they can keep some of your things during the interview and pick them later. Do this in a respectful manner and never bug them.

As soon as you enter the room, *greet every person with a smile, and offer your hand for a firm handshake* (if applicable, some culture doesn't do handshakes). Ask them how they are and start with a little small talk. I usually use the "weather topic" during small talk.

The last interview I had, I talked about the cold winter transitioning to spring and summer. "It's still cold outside, I can't wait for summer." I started. The interviewer agreed, and I don't know how, but we ended up talking about our winter experiences and our respective families.

If this happened to you, when you and the interviewer started a conversation outside the interview itself, this is a plus point for you. *Some applicants are hired not because they answered all the questions right, but because they build a "brand" through a conversation.*

Your interviewer upon assessing all the candidates might see your application and remember, *"I like this guy, he was the one who was looking forward to summer, and I enjoyed talking to him."* This for sure will give you a higher chance.

The **Body of the Interview** is the main event. The interviewers will be asking questions, and you will do most of the talking. On average, this will be about fifteen minutes of question and answer exchanges.

As an insider tip: Most of my interviews are on questionnaires being read by the interviewer. This means that there will be one set of the same questions for all the applicants. If you were asked about your weaknesses, then for sure all the applicants will have the same questions. During the interview, they take note of your answers. Some questionnaires have point systems which I will be discussing later.

Given that all applicants have the same questions, what would make you different from the rest will help you stand out. This is called your "branding." How you portray yourself, answer the questions, and the consistency of your answers will help you build your brand. Remember that if you have a "brand" you will be unforgettable. The reason why I was called Mr. Customer Service with a big smile during a mock interview was that I portrayed a smiley guy with knowledge of customer service. Later in the book, you will learn how to project, answer your questions and be consistent.

The **Closing** is the last part of the interview. This will conclude the whole process. You will know that you are still doing well in the interview if after all the questions in the questionnaire have been asked, you and the interviewer/s are still conversing about lots of stuff. This will only happen if you answer the last interview question, "Do you have any questions for us?"

My last interview experience, I had at least two questions asked which brought about more conversation. I had wrapped up the session, and as I was walking out the door, they still asked me some more trivial stuff that we are interested in. I knew then that they were interested in having me, and I made sure that my answers would convey my interest in the job. Yes, I was hired shortly after that interview.

2. Smile, Listen, and Answer—Verbal Communication 101

You can showcase your communication skills during the interview. Remember that communication is interaction. It is an exchange of ideas or messages from one person to the other person. During an interview, all of the elements of your communication skills are being evaluated. How you respond, what you respond, and how your body is responding to what you are saying. Since it is a shared interaction between two people, it is important that you receive their message (questions, clarifications, responses), and you convey your message back appropriately.

For the vocal and verbal elements of communication, these are my tips:

Five Ways to Improve and Effectively Utilize Your Verbal Communication Skills in a Job Interview

1. Listen to understand.

Have you met someone who steals the limelight?

I have. They are the people who like to be the star of the show, whatever it takes. How do you feel about it?

I know that during the interview, you are the star of the show—or you are assumed to be. But a great conversationalist makes everybody stars of the show. A limelight stealer—which you should not be (in an interview or in an everyday conversation)—is a poor listener.

How do you know someone is a limelight stealer? Take this for example: you started a conversation to share something about yourself. You want somebody to listen to you. However, if the person you are talking to suddenly shifts the conversation from your perspective onto his own story that doesn't really relate to what you said, then in your head you'll just say, "Here he goes again."

In an interview, you don't talk. You respond. By all means, during the introduction you can start a conversation after the *Hello, how are you part;* but try not to steal the show. You are conversing, so you can listen to what they say and importantly respond to what they are saying.

LIMELIGHT STEALER

You: It's so warm outside, summer is here. It's a good day!

Interviewer: It is. I don't really like summer, though.

You: You don't? I like summer. I love summer. I actually planned my whole summer with vacations, visits to beaches, museum visits blah blah blah.

Just so you know, they don't really care as there has been no personal relationship built during your first ten minutes of meeting.

A GOOD RESPONDER

You: It's so warm outside, summer is here. It's a good day!

Interviewer: It is. I don't really like summer, though.

You: Are you a winter person?

Interviewer: Yes, I am.

You: You must love winter activities, skiing, and going skating?

Interviewer: Yes, I do. I usually ski at Mont Leblanc every winter. I love the sport.

You: That place is so nice. Don't you think?

Interviewer: I agree. It has been blah blah blah blah

I know you don't really care, but you should. When they tell you more, you're doing a good job. You're making them the star of the show. They feel good about themselves, and it is becoming a lovely day. This is again a brand-building strategy.

Of course, you can't do this hack on a panel of four. When more than one person in involved, it could be a challenge, but you can start a conversation where everyone can be involved—like the interview room set up. Remember, you have to respond accordingly. One more point to remember: conversation can become personal, but you must respond professionally.

Furthermore, active listening helps you answer the interview questions. Remember that the first question and your answer to that question will bring up the follow-up questions. Follow-up questions are as important as the main question. These include the interviewer asking you to clarify your answers, explore more of what you know, and dig deep on your personality. This is when attentive listening is valuable.

During the main event, the limelight will shift from everybody to yourself. In this instance, make sure that you make them feel involved in the show. How do you do this? No, don't try to ask them questions back; instead, you can do this by addressing everybody and by looking at them. You answer either by telling your story or giving insights that are persuasive and convincing. If you see them nodding their heads or reacting positively (smiling), you're doing a great job.

2. The Voice

I don't like my speaking voice. I think that I am part of the majority who doesn't like their own voice. What is important though is not the voice but the message. What's more amazing is how we can actually command our voice to sound the way we want it.

One thing that I have learned from one of the personality development workshops I attended is that we can portray how we want to communicate. Imagine our vocal element has levels 1-10. Level 1 as the gentle side and level 10 as the aggressive side of verbal communicating. The levels in between are the progression.

For example, our daily conversations with friends will demand a level 5-6. Depending on your personality, you may be on the meek side or the aggressive side. However, you can turn your notch to a higher or lower level as appropriate. In an interview, for example, you can determine what level the interviewers are. You can start at levels 5-6. It is recommended to at least mirror the level of communication of your interviewer.

Besides controlling the level of your vocals, modulating your voice is essential too. Modulation is when you regulate the softness and loudness of your voice. This technique helps you emphasize the statement you want to convey. This can also help you deliver positive energy.

Talking about vocal elements, let's learn from singers. The importance of vocalizations and facial muscle stretching on speaking. This is especially true for those of us whose English is the second language—our tongue twists unexpectedly which results in either stuttering, mumbling or slurring. When you condition your facial muscles (tongue and lips included) this will help with the proper enunciation of words.

3. Breathe in, breathe out...

Breathing calms the nerves. Do not forget your slow, deep breathing exercises before your interview. More importantly, don't forget to breathe during the interview. Remember that if you don't breathe, it constricts your vessels. This constriction will make you gasp for air and grasp for ideas. Breathing dilates your vessels thus allowing for continuous blood flow and oxygen. This makes your brain more functional thus ideas flow, and interview answers are on hand.

Also, it is important to be aware of how we answer questions. I tend to talk fast and soft when my ideas are flowing continuously during a conversation. Unfortunately, due to my accent and excitement, most of what I say is unclear. During an interview, I make sure that I pause, I breathe, and I modulate my voice.

4. Keep it simple, sweet, and significant

Before you go to your interview, make sure that you collect all your stories, and you know yourself well, so you can gather your thoughts enough to answer their questions.

Keep your group of words simple. One thing I have noticed between a native and a non-native English speaker is the use of words in sentences. Having primarily studied English in school through reading and writing, we usually utilize words in a literary way and not in a conversational way. The fact of the matter is, you do not have to impress the interviewer with your English vocabulary by using high falutin words but impress them with your answers. Use simple conversational English and use technical terms if applicable. We communicate to express and not to impress.

Keep it sweet. Modulate your responses in a respectful manner. Make sure you talk in a way that you can hear what you are saying, and you are keeping the proper pace to respond. Do not forget to breathe and modulate your voice when speaking.

Keep your answers substantial. You don't have all the time in the world to explain yourself in front of the interviewer. Make sure you respect all of your time by answering the questions directly, then supporting with four to five supporting sentences. If you need to tell a story, make sure you have fully developed your story so that neither you nor the panel will be lost in it. Remember that the more significant your answers are, the better the brand you are building.

5. Always speak positivity.

Remember that during your interview, you have to build your brand. At the end of the day, everybody should feel good. One thing that you can do is to use affirmative and positive words. Responses with optimism make everybody in the room feel good. If the question warrants a negative answer like describing your weaknesses, either make it a point that it will end on a positive note like what you have learned or how you are managing your weaknesses.

Do not give negative impressions to any character of your stories. If you are asked about conflict resolution, and you want to tell the story of your hot-headed colleagues, refrain from using negative adjectives. Instead, explain how your colleagues became hot-tempered during the situation.

If you are asked about your last employer, and why are you planning to change workplaces, do not describe the bad side of the workplace no matter how you hate it. Always be reminded that whatever you say, reflects your attitude.

3. Action speaks louder than words

We all know the fact that in communication, what we say is important and how we say it is also a significant factor. In fact, many studies have suggested that proper use of non-verbal cues creates an effective communicator. More than spoken words and voice quality, we must be aware of how we deliver our message. I also tell my friends that an interview, whether it is a job or an exam, is a performance.

Let's take, for example, one of the most important non-verbal cues during an interview which not everyone is comfortable with: eye contact. I am not comfortable with eye contact, and it is culture-based. Most of the western countries believe that it is respectful if you maintain some eye contact while you are having a conversation. Most Asians, however, including myself, treat direct eye contact as disrespectful, especially if you are talking to someone in a higher position.

Even to this day, I struggle with making eye contact. However, during an interview, you have to perform as a respectful individual in a different environment. Given the cultural context like here in Canada, people prefer comfortable eye contact while conversing. It may not be comfortable for you but remember you are performing a role that will help you get the job.

Does performing mean faking it? Do you have to be not yourself during the interview? No. First, the interviewer will notice if you are being unreal. Second, effective use of non-verbal cues reflects your communication skills and not your acting abilities. Last, if you want to convey your message, it is essential that you learn how to deliver it effectively.

4. Ask and you shall receive: the interview.

The interview is the main event of the day. Although impressions start as soon as you enter the room, most of the evaluation depends on how you respond to the interview questions. How will you make a difference? How will they remember you?

During this phase, you will also have the chance to get to know your employer personally. Hopefully, you did your research before the day of the interview. You get bonus points if you know something about the company—and you showcase this knowledge during the interview.

Four Types of Healthcare Interview Questions

Having experienced being interviewed and been to workshops and learning about the interview structure here in Canada, I can categorize healthcare interview questions into four types: the **common questions, direct questions, implied questions, and closing questions.**

- **Common questions**—these are the questions that we hear being asked at the majority of interviews. These include those questions which ask about yourself, your expected salary, and your insights about your experience and other workplace issues (e.g., conflict management). These questions are best answered by your own personal work experience. It takes good self-awareness for this to fly.

- **Direct questions**—these demand direct answers. This is not limited to questions answerable with a yes or no, but it also includes questions about your nursing skills—the technical questions. Example of these questions include, "Why did you specialize in OR nursing?", "Do you like working in a team?", "What will you do if you found your client on the floor, unconscious?"

    Remember to answer all questions in a complete sentence and with a complete thought. Support your answers with two or three more sentences. If applicable, you can integrate your experience in your answers.

- **Implied questions**—these are abstract questions. Answering these questions gives them insights into your personal beliefs, philosophies, and values. Questions like "What motivates you?", "How do you see yourself in 10 years?", "What are your strengths and weaknesses?" "How do you handle criticism." To answer this, you need foresight, and this is also an opportunity to show your attitude towards yourself, the people around you, and your work.

- **Closing question**—the trickiest question. Before the interview ends, they will ask you, "Do you have any question for us?" Almost always, we want to say "no" and leave the room. However, this is not recommended. This question can be your opportunity to once again present your interest in the job. One suggestion I gather is to ask questions that will seem beneficial to them. For example, you can ask, "I am interested in research, and this institution is onto research, how do you support your staff with regards to research participation?" With that question, the company becomes the highlight of the conversation.

It may be tempting to ask when you will know if you will be hired but refrain from asking this. This question does not say anything positive about you except your interest for your own sake. It is not bad, but the closing question does not mean the end of the interview. Like my last interview, after the closing question, we spent a good ten minutes discussing other details of the job. If things get more comfortable between you and the interviewer, this could be a better opportunity to ask about the hiring process.

***

"How do you handle conflicts with coworkers?" she asked me.

"I talk to the person involved," I answered. "I have been in a professional conflict before with my other colleagues, and it is important to always be professional. For example, I remember a time when the shift before me had neglected to set up the room for our next surgical case. Before their shift ended, I asked the team leader what happened during the shift and why it was left undone. Hearing his explanation, which did not seem to be reasonable, I told him that I was disappointed. I reminded him of our policies and routines, and possible setbacks due to the neglect. We came to an understanding, and we both learned from that day. He is a friend, but we must maintain professionalism in the workplace."

One of the questions I have answered during my last interview.

***

Anyone who is going to be interviewed should study the common interview questions and how to answer them. Their guidelines are helpful to all job seekers. But we should keep in mind that these are just guidelines and should not be used to answer a real interview question. The reason behind is because it is a general answer that will never make you stand out from the others. Imagine if everybody who is asked the same question, answers with the same thought as the guideline. Which answer will the hiring manager remember?

The one who shared a great story and the one with the highest score is the memorable.

Later, I will tell you about having the highest score. First, I will share the techniques I have been using and have learned from the different workshops I have attended that will for sure create your brand during your interview.

The 4 S in Answering Interview Questions that Builds your Brand

1. **Story/ Situation. Your story is unique to you.**

   This is one of the most important things to remember when answering interview questions. If it is applicable, tell a story. Tell YOUR story. The most related stories and most relatable will always be remembered. As Tyrion Lannister quoted in the series finale of Game of Thrones, "There's nothing more powerful in the world than a good story."

   If you give the interviewer an interesting one, this may spark more conversations. Also, this will build your brand since your story will show the values you have by delivering your insights on your given situation. Sometimes, your story is your brand. Make sure, of course, that your story answers the question.

2. **Substance/ eSSence. Make it short and clear.**

   Answer the question. Give supporting details. Emphasized the "message" you want to convey. Tie up your story.

   Refrain from giving excessive details. You don't have to explain everything. Giving unnecessary details will give confusion. Sometimes, you get lost on the thought content when you give too many details, especially when you're not prepared.

3. **Skills/ Experience. Showcase the skill you applied by stating from your own experience.**

   You don't tell a story that will not highlight your skills—that would be a waste. How did you resolve conflict? You talked to the person involved. It showcases your self-management skills and your conflict resolution skills. Your story is the icing on the cake. Your skills are the cake.

If asked about how you can handle pressure at work, you don't answer "very well." Answer with your story that if pressure means time constraints, you've been involved in projects that are time-sensitive, like creating policies for a year-end quality management meeting. During this time, you planned and organized to ensure deadlines were met.

In the example above, you just showcased your time management and organizational skills. Also, you have established the fact that you are involved in policymaking, quality management meeting, and other responsibilities that it may benefit your organization.

Additionally, if the question demands a technical answer which is usually related to the environment wherein you are applying, answer the questions based on the standard of practice. If asked, "How do you manage a patient with measles who is from a different cultural background than yours?"

If you have this experience, then you can tell your story ensuring what you did is the standard of care (which I hope you did). If not, then base your answer on knowledge of the case, the standards, and your personal values, answer the question strategically.

Insider's Tip: This type of question can be answered in general and specific. The general answer involves your precautions, reporting, nursing process, nursing care, and your personal values. Specific involves where you are applying, which means that if you are applying as an ER nurse, you should answer the question like an ER nurse. If you are applying to work on the floor, then nursing management on the floor is what you must tell them about.

What if you don't have experience or a story to share? No conflicts in the workplace you have resolved or witnessed that had resolved? Your last option is your personal experience. You could share conflict resolution with your basketball team, with a family member, or your other job unrelated to what you have right now. Use this with caution and don't make it so personal that it will make everybody in the room uncomfortable. The last resort will be a theoretical answer, wherein what would you have done, if a certain type of conflict arises. The majority of the applicants will use this, and hopefully you will have one distinct answer from the rest.

4. **Solution/ Results. Make sure the story ends with resolution or a positive result.**

   Never let your interviewer ask what happens next. I know it is a great way to know if they really are hooked in your story, but you don't want them to leave hanging. Nobody likes that. Make your story interesting, and they will look forward to how it ends.

   Wrap it up nicely. You have stated the problem in your story (*You had conflict with a colleague*). You tell them your ways on how you solve the problem. (*You have talked to your colleague stating the skillset you used. On this example, it is micromanagement and conflict resolution*). The result of your solution should end the story (*There is an understanding between you and your colleague, and everybody was reminded of what are the things that need to be done.*)

   Always and I cannot emphasize this enough, share a feel-good story. The interview should end so that everybody feels good about themselves. One failed interview I had, I already knew I wouldn't get the job since I felt awful after it. I made necessary preparations—I thought—and I looked forward to it since that was a big break. If only

I knew how the system worked back then, I could have been more prepared, or I'll say essentially prepared for this.

5. **Bonus Insider Tip. S number 5. Score.**

Siderails. I was asked about side rails/bedrails. In the OR and recovery where I had my six years of experience, side rails are used for safety. I would have been correct with that answer if not asked about it on a geriatric floor with clients with dementia. Apparently, on this floor, side rails are a safety concern—even a health risk. According to studies, there are bedrail injuries, entrapment, and even deaths among aged people. Some consider it as an assistive device, others a restraint. I fell short on my interview question score. I did not get the job.

Most of my interviews for jobs in health care facilities and hospitals are score-based. This makes sense since this will make it possible to come to an objective decision regarding the applicants. The higher the score, the better. Your story and brand affect your interviewers' emotions, but you don't want to forget the objective factor.

My personal experience above is one of the highlights of this book. If you have the chance to get an interview on a medical floor, make sure that you know the cases on the medical floor and review your standards of practice, your nursing management, and the common cases you will meet on the floor.

"We often do pyloromyotomy, what do you know about pyloric stenosis?" she asked me. This time, I have learned, and I came prepared. If I have to ace this operating room job interview in a pediatric hospital, I should learn the OR standards by heart, should familiar myself with pediatric surgical cases, and know my nursing management of pediatric patients in the operating room. Confession:

I answered the question wrong, but the whole interview made more sense, and I felt good after the conversation.

Studying about the specialty of the area you are applying to seems like a no-brainer for us nurses. I thought it was probably just me who knew nothing about how this works. It was not until an old colleague from the Philippines paid me a visit and shared the same experience that I realized the pervasiveness of this issue. He had an interview for a surgical floor nursing job and asked about post-surgical nursing management. He came unprepared for this. He did not get the job, but he learned from it.

His next interviews involved many nursing questions, and in some, he actually had to interpret ECG readings. He got hired.

The juice here is that you need to be prepared enough to be both subjective and objective question. If there is one thing that you can pick from this portion of the book, that is study the area where you want to practice your nursing.

PLEASE DO NOT FORGET TO THANK THE INTERVIEWER FOR THE OPPORTUNITY AND THEIR TIME.

5. The Stronger Things: The PPIPF Elements

A successful job interview does not happen during the interview. The most important day for applicants booked for interview are the days before it. From the moment you receive the call up to your interview day, you must gather the stronger things. I call these the PPIPF elements: Planning and Preparation, Impression, Practice, and Follow up. (No pun intended).

PLANNING

How do you plan and prepare? Usually, you are given two weeks' notice. I don't know how you feel when you receive the call. But if you really like the job offered, you are most likely excited, marking your calendar to remind yourself, and googling "how to ace your interview"—which of course is part of planning. What else do you have to do? Here is my checklist:

- ☐ Mark your calendar—or calendars if you have more. I know I have mentioned this above, but to emphasize its significance, I will tell you again to not forget this important appointment. Write on an actual calendar. Put it on your phone calendar and set a reminder. Of course, add the date, time, and place. Before I forget, when you receive a call for an interview, you can ask the person on the line to hold for a sec so you can grab a pen and paper. In retrospect, if you are expecting this kind of call, make sure you have pen and paper around where you are. Write on the paper, the date, time and place and clarify any details. If they can send the notice to your email, it would be better. Why am I focusing on this? I think I missed a great opportunity one time when I forgot the time of my interview. Heartbreaking.

- ☐ Plan what to wear. Dress to impress. What you wear for an interview speaks volume about your interest in the job. I have a hard time dressing up for occasions. I'm a T-shirt, pants, and a cap guy and that's it. We don't wear suits in the Philippines either. Formal/business attire for me is a long sleeve polo. Wearing suits make me feel awkward. For the sake of getting the dream job, suit it is, and I do my best to make myself comfortable wearing it.

I remember how during one of the mock interviews at a workshop I was participating in, I wore my formal long sleeve polo and black pants since wearing suits feel awkward for me. I got hired in the mock interview, but I earned a low grade in the attire part. It may not seem significant, but I think it does affect how they see you, and of course how you project yourself. Comfortable attire—comfort. Comfortable wearing formal attire for an interview—confidence.

- Search the web for the most common interview questions and try to write a draft of how you would answer the question with your stories. I hope you don't forget that as much as possible, share relevant personal stories that answer the interview question. At this point, you can gather your stories in your memory, know yourself more, and collect all the words that you can say during the interview. For us non-native English speakers, running out of words is common, so plan. Write and read it aloud. This is a great opportunity to edit your story, clarify the context, omit insignificant details.

- Research the company's mission, vision, philosophy, and latest updates. From this research, you can gear yourself up for the tricky closing question. Plan for your question.

- Learn about the job you are applying for. You have to read over the job posting if it is still available, if not, you can search for the job description of the job you are applying for. Take note of the acronyms that may be unfamiliar to you and make yourself familiar. Make sure that if they require a certificate (for example CPR), you have it gathered as a proof.

- Research the nursing setting you are applying for. If you are applying for a nursing home for an aged population, study the population group and their nursing care and management, cases, and issues involving their care and environment.

- ☐ Acquaint yourself with the Canadian workplace. If this is your first job as a newcomer, I highly suggest you find workshops/events/groups/person that will explain to you the workplace scenario in Canada and health sector.

- ☐ Make sure you get a good rest the day before the interview. As much as possible, reduce your stress a few days before the interview. Always be positive.

PREPARATION

The difference between planning and preparing is the action taken. In planning, everything is happening in the mind. During preparation, you are doing what you have planned. From the above checklist, you just have to take action. Have a dress rehearsal. See yourself in the mirror and tell yourself it suits what you're wearing. Search and write what you search. This is like a real-life assignment.

IMPRESSION

Build an impression that lasts. You're a nurse. By nature, you are a likable individual. Be like one during your interview. Basic things to remember:

- ✓ Be confident in carrying yourself
- ✓ Wear that big smile
- ✓ Give a firm handshake
- ✓ Arrive 15 minutes before the interview time. Not more than, and please do not be late.
- ✓ Make sure you have fresh breath and neutral body scent.

- ✓ Always be respectful.
- ✓ Be mindful with the tone of your voice and the expressions of your face.
- ✓ Don't make extra hand gestures that may create distractions.
- ✓ Use positive words always.
- ✓ Be mindful of your posture.
- ✓ Create a day that starts positively.

PRACTICE

Have you been to a speaking engagement before? Or maybe a school reporting? Or just your first date. Do you remember what you did before the "big" day arrived? Yes. You practiced.

Let's take, for example, your first date. You want to impress the person whom you asked or have asked you for a date since you like her/him. From the day you agreed on a date up to the day before the date, you have been wondering how the day will look like. Will you shake her hand when you arrive? Firm handshakes, perhaps? Or you will reach out and give her a small hug? Are you going to offer her a seat like what you see a movie? I know you get me. This is the same as having an interview: You picture your day, and you practice your ways.

The following practice tips are more effective if you have someone whom you trust to check on you. If none is available to do so, a mirror will do.

- Dress rehearsal is important. Wear that dress or that suit and walk with it. Practice the best way to sit on the chair.
- Practice your smile and your handshake. Ask the person you chose if it looks and feels natural.

- Practice answering questions. Read your answers aloud and listen to what you are saying. If it sounds bad, it probably is. Memorize your answers by heart, it shouldn't be hard since it is your story. Ask a friend to do a mock interview with you.

- Practice hand gestures and body gestures. Watch people like Barrack Obama to see how he talks and acts. Watch how influential people respond to questions and study their actions. Imitate them. Remember you are influencing the person in front of you to choose you as the right candidate.

- Practice being grateful. Practice your tone of voice. Record your voice, and ask someone to listen to it, ask for feedback and modulate it accordingly.

FOLLOW UP

After the interview, allow at least three days to send a follow-up letter. This part of the hiring process is new to me as a newcomer. However, it seems to be standard practice here in Canada. I don't know how much of an impact the follow-up letter has, but for sure it is a great way to say once again that you are grateful for the opportunities given to you. Since I really wanted the job I applied for, I wrote a follow-up/ thank you letter. If you're going to do this, be sure to include highlights of your interview as a reminder of your conversations.

My assessment sheet when I did the mock interview in Career Transition Program for IMDs. Take note of the criteria on how they score us. This is a helpful guide and reminder during your interview.

The Surest Way to Find a Job in Canada: My Powerful Six Tips

I can't help but to share over and over my story of how I obtained my first job here in Canada as a personal support worker and an unregulated care provider. It has been the core of my professional experience in this new country. For those who have not read yet, I got my first job from a referral of someone whom I don't know. She was my aunt's friend, whom she befriended on her daily bus commute to work.

I don't know about you, but this amazes me. From that moment on, it's not just my life that had changed, but it rippled to many lives around me. If you're reading this, it affected you too. This is not possible without that day. I thank God for it.

That was my first job application and my first job interview. Needless to say (but I'm saying it anyway) that I was hired since I already told you that it was my first job as a landed immigrant. It opened doors to many opportunities and growth. The reason why I want to share these six powerful tips with you to ensure that you get your ideal job here in Canada and may this help you open many other doors of opportunity and ripples to all the people who surround you.

Disclaimer: These tips are especially helpful for those who are in Canada. For those who are not, this can be helpful and/or may be applicable. Just read on.

1. Networking.

If you're tired of reading the same "networking" word throughout this book, my blogs or vlogs; I'm sorry, that's the only way I can emphasize the significance of going outside and meet new people. Of course, I don't mean meeting random people at the mall, although that might help. I don't mean tindering either. What I would suggest is for you to participate in events (paid or free) or go to places where you think you will meet people who are as like-minded as you are.

Mind you, since I arrived in Canada, I had been participating in many networking workshops, events, and simple gatherings. Not to mention that I consider myself as an introvert. The best thing about Canada, Ottawa in particular, is that there are lots of networking events. How I survived these networking events despite being an introvert? I smile.

Through these events, I have met people who have taught me how to compete in employment, business, and self-growth. I have also helped people who are looking for jobs and motivation to pursue what they want. All because I tried to talk to people. It's not my nature, but it is a survival thing.

If you think that I probably have lots of people in my network, you're wrong. I don't think I know more than 30 people here in Ottawa, aside from my relatives. I know a few people, but these few people have amazing networks. Find key persons.

How will you start building a network or looking for one? I started looking online—the introverted way. However, the better way, I guess, is to look for a place where people with the same interest as you go. The perfect example is joining a church community—if it suits your belief.

Can you imagine if you met me (a shy type) at one of these churches? I have 30 people behind me as my network. Meet five shy type people, and your network grows exponentially. These networks believe it or not know of job openings for sure. Interestingly, if you're lucky enough, you won't only get a job opening opportunity but also a referral! I probably have referred and recommended at least five people. My referral has given them the job they wanted or have helped them pursue more for their careers. Again, just me, the shy type.

Never underestimate the power of meeting the right strangers. Be critical for sure. You have to feel that this new person will contribute to your growth. You will know them by listening to the stories they share. The words that come out of their mouths. I know it is wrong to judge a person on your first meeting or based on the stories they shared. But be wise.

I will tell you one secret how I determined a better person from a good person: a good person talks about himself, his accomplishments and other people—making him look better than the others. A better person, ask things about you (your goals in particular and not personal things that creates gossips), listens to you, and share his stories. His stories usually coming from his struggles and how he succeeded. He shares the stories of others as a lesson he had learned from them, or as an inspiration to help you. He uses positive and encouraging words. At the end of the conversation, a better person will make you feel better about life. A good person ends the conversation by feeling good about himself.

No. There's no bad person. I only consider a bad person if that person does not share a story. You wouldn't know, you might meet someone (let's call her Jen for our purposes) at some of these gatherings.

2. Preparation.

After meeting Jen at the gathering and telling you that she might know of a job you would be a good fit for, she called and told you that you should submit your resume online. All applicants to their company must go through an online application screening process. She also tells you that the job posted online will be down tomorrow evening, so you have to send in an application as soon as possible.

If this scenario happens today, how prepared are you?

Is your resume up to date? Would you have time to tailor your resume according to the job opening? Do you have a ready to go cover letter?

We don't know when opportunity knocks. I have a ready to go resume and cover letter which I check and update if need be. With or without me planning to look for another job, I know that my resume is ready to go.

Make sure that your papers are ready, especially if you are actively looking for a job. This reduces your stress, and this gives you more mental security.

You might think since Jen referred you for the job, there are also bonus points in screening. Unless Jen is the hiring manager, she has no say regarding whether your resume will push through so always ace your resume writing. If Jen is indeed the hiring manager, most professional jobs have more than one person to screen you. Don't embarrass Jen with your poorly written resume.

3. **Presentation.**

How you present yourself is your brand. Your brand is how your prospective employer remembers you. Make sure they remember you in a positive way.

If you're lucky to get an interview, arrive on the scene as someone who shows them that you are serious about this job. Let them remember you as someone with a pleasing personality. The one whose values relate to the company's value and someone whom they enjoy talking to.

I remembered when I did my interview workshop, the "pretend" employer remembered me in two ways: having a nice smile and Mr. customer service.

It is not bad if the managers during their deliberation saw your name and remembered, "He was the immigrant with a nice tie, and very respectful on his answers.."

There are no pretensions on presenting yourself in an interview. You just can't pretend to be someone who is not you. Once you walk in the room, you need to project that you are the right person for the job, and under your wings are the qualifications ready to be presented.

I say this because people may misunderstand the concept as faking it. It is not. Although faking may get you through, the true persona will eventually reveal itself during the interview or in the workplace. Do not pretend you speak French if you don't. Do not pretend you have five years of experience if you don't.

Believe in your qualifications and experience. Know yourself—strengths, weaknesses, goals, and values because this is the core of your interview. You are your brand. If you can't make your personality lovable at least make it likable.

4. Optimism.

If Jen is a good worker and she recommended you to her boss, the chances of you getting hired are 60%. If you did well during your interview and they like you, the chances of you getting hired are 90%. The numbers have no statistical evidence, just based on my experience.

The 10% of uncertainty comes from having a good reference, timing and unforeseen circumstances like you don't want the job anymore. The waiting from the day of your interview and the next call from the employer is dreadful. During this time, be as positive as you can. Remember to send a follow-up email. Pray a lot and contemplate what happened.

I have experienced a few job rejections. Some of them I did not expect, and some I did. I have one big job interview that I knew I wouldn't get, but it was the turning point of my next interview experience. It gave me insights on what to do next. That day inspired me to create this book, too. Share what I learned from preparing incorrectly.

As we know, optimism can only get as far as trying to manifest a positive result. But what really creates better growth is the change of perspective. We don't always get a positive result, but a change in how we see things can still create a positive product. Seeing beyond rejections and still creating a positive impact is key.

5. Make it a habit to do your best on opportunities that harness your skills and attitude.

I always recommend networking. That's for sure a great way to meet people and build connections. Besides events, networking also happens when you decide to go to school, attend informal learning seminars, your course consolidations, and doing your survival job(s).

I am enjoying my present job right now as an operating room nurse in a Children's hospital. This wouldn't be possible if I had not done well during my consolidation in the same hospital. I have used my nursing background to showcase my skills, and I tried very much to get along with everybody. The nursing staff recommended me to the manager, to add to this, two surgeons whom I have worked with during the one-month consolidation, commended me to the manager. I had no plans for impressing everybody. I just did my best. But if it comes naturally to you—doing your best—every time, it wouldn't be difficult to impress people. Remember, people are watching you.

Moreover, I have good references from my former bosses and charge nurses. My former manager doesn't usually give a reference, but since I did well while working on my job, she had seen the growth that I ought to have. I am very thankful for that.

If given an opportunity to work with other people, do your job well. Respect each and every one, and always be positive towards relating to others. Relationships are key to networking.

6. Help a friend.

I don't know if you believe in karma or quantum physics, but I do. If you've got a job partly because Jen helped you, then you have to pay it forward, not because the society forced you to, but because you owe it to Jen to extend the help she gave to you. You should keep the ripples flowing.

Circumstances will give you the opportunity to meet people whom you are able to help. Help them. Do what Jen did. Be the better person during the gathering. The more people you help, the more help and good karma you will receive in return. This is one absolute law of the world. We should be helping each other. There are lots of opportunities for everybody. Help them find theirs.

I help people if I have the opportunity; and I believe that good karma is on my side, as I pursue the growth that I have been wanting. I want to see you growing so that you have no choice but to extend help. Nobody grows exponentially without extending their hands.

What Happens on Your First Day at Work in Canada? A Tale of All My Firsts in Canada

My brother-in-law was delighted that I'd got the job but warned me, "You might find everything here fast-paced. Brace yourself." During that time, I was unsure what he meant by fast-paced. All I ever wanted was to start a job. In fact, I had been waiting for two months since landing in Ottawa.

First Day with Pay—Pay per Work

My new job as an unregulated care provider and personal support worker in a retirement home started with paperwork. My boss handed me thick folders of policies and protocols to read, trainings and quizzes to answer, and other mandated reading materials given by the government of Canada, province of Ontario and or the company.

I suppose all jobs start with orientation. The good news here is that here in Canada, the pay starts once the orientation starts. I was happy. I was paid to read. Surely this wasn't the fast pace my brother-in-law was talking about. I made sure I read slowly and understood every detail. Why not? I am paid per hour.

My pay started at 12.50CAD/hr. during my probation period. I remembered I asked my boss about this when she decided to hire me as part-time. She was shy to tell me how much pay I would be receiving since it's close to minimum wage (in 2014) for a job that is almost nursing. However, I didn't mind. Twelve dollars and fifty cents per hour sounded good to me, especially when you see that 24 cans of coke costs only to about eight dollars; I was that naïve, and that job was the best thing that happened to me in three months.

This introduced me to the concept of pay per hour work. In the Philippines, most employees are paid on fix dates (15th and last day of the month, on weekdays). Since most workers are full time, you can expect a more-or-less-fixed income.

In Canada, most employees are paid per hour. Employment ranges from being full-time, part-time or casual. An 8-hour shift usually gives you 7.5 hours of pay since most employees are entitled to 30 minutes of uninterrupted break. Part-timers and casual employees calculate their salaries based on how many hours they have worked in two weeks. Payout happens every two weeks or bi-weekly.

These were all new concepts to me as a newcomer. If in two weeks, I have four full shifts (7.5hrs) and one short shift (5hr), my total hours of work is 35 hours. With my 12.50CAD/hr. pay, I can expect a GROSS pay of CAD437.50. If all taxes and dues are deducted, you will expect your net pay to be more or less CAD350—if I'm generous.

This new reality made me realized why most workers I know in Canada have at least two jobs. This is because more hours of work give you more pay. One part-time job has limited working hours. However, more working hours will only give you better pay if you are paid more per hour.

The reason I decided to better myself and pursue growth in my career was that I believed that the more growth you achieved, the more responsibilities you could handle, the more help you could render, thus the more returns you would receive.

First Day Working with Colleagues

After a day of paperwork, my orientation continued to job shadowing. I had to watch the staff to see what they do and eventually help them as the day progressed. I had a few morning and evening shifts that happened over those two weeks. Then I was off to do my first solo shift.

Being an unregulated care provider (UCP) in a retirement home setting has its own definition of nursing. It is daunting at first until you become familiar with your routines. My first shift alone was a short shift. This means that after I received a report, I would organize the oral medications due for the clients in the building, see them, assess if need be and report to in-charge staff if we find anything beyond normal.

The challenge here is the organization and time management. Short shift UCP has more clients to give meds since they seldom do documentation, assessment, and they are not in charge of the service. They basically just pass medications and do vital signs if delegated.

Then my first day as a staff in charge happened. Some retirement homes have their UCPs in charge of the nursing service. It was my fourth week in the job. As a part-timer who only comes Tuesday, Thursday and every other weekend, and picking up some shifts, I was not an everyday person. I have all the excuses in my mind that I couldn't be in charge, because I don't think I can. My manager reassured me that she'll be available in case I need support. She was helpful, but still, I am not confident. This was the fast-paced experience, I thought. Few days of orientation, few shifts of work, then be in charge. A transition I had not experienced before.

There is no way we can find out that we can do it until we do it. Everything is a learning curve.

First Day of Fall—Not the Season, But A Person

I lifted a gentleman once from the floor when he fell, when our policy states that we can't lift—which I learned after the fact. I thought I was helping him when I realized I was risking myself and the client's safety. It was my first time seeing someone on the floor and asking for my help to lift him up. It was my PSW shift, and this first encounter had given me loads of lessons whenever you find a resident on the floor. Things to do includes asking for additional help, assessing the client, making the client comfortable, knowing your lifting policies, if client can help himself/herself lift with support, staff can support as per policy, if not then call for paramedics to help lift. Ensure client is in the most comfortable position, warm and hemodynamically stable. That was our policy, so I advise you to not just read slowly on your orientation paper works but understand too.

First Day Someone Complained About My Job

For the first time in my career, someone complained about me and said that I didn't know what I was doing. Being the new face in a place where routine is master for clients, it is important to build rapport. It was my first PSW shift as an orientee when one resident called me out for not doing my job right. Good thing I have my colleague by my side and reassuring him that what I have been doing was the proper way. If you wonder what the task is, it is lifting his feet on his bed and removing his socks. He was not convinced though that I did a good job. I have reported what happened to my charge nurse and she advised me to document it on his chart. My boss heard the complain the next day and talked to me about it. I wrote an incident report, my colleague who was with me backed me up, and eventually, the resident apologized for what happened and stated that his foot was sore that night and should have been patient for a newbie. Everybody was happy.

We learned how crucial documentation in nursing. What is done or not done, if undocumented is unsupported. In Canada, all interventions or incident are documented. How everything was reported, how assessment was done, how health teachings were given, how options are laid to residents, how their choices are made, how refusal of care was verbalized—everything that you did and any significant event during your shift. This will save you a ton of headaches in the future.

First Day Someone Appreciated My Job and Gave Me A Winter Jacket

To build rapport with clients, the best way to do it is to listen to what they are saying. Respond in a way that they will tell you more about themselves. Share a little about yourself too, as this will build trust. People are interested in people. They want to know the people around them. I guess I did something right when one resident decided to give her blue winter jacket (unisex) to me. She assumed that as a newcomer, I probably don't have winter stuff. I was delighted because it was a very nice jacket. I took the jacket, but I told my manager about it.

My manager was not sure how to react. We both know that we aren't supposed to receive gifts from our clients. There are lots of legal possibilities that might happen to me. Although it was voluntarily given, circumstances may change. I understood what she was saying. Later that shift, I gave the jacket back. I was happy about being appreciated. The resident was not delighted about me giving it back, but she understood.

Don't let your emotions dictate your judgment. Remember that we work in a place where there are standards and protocol. Always be mindful of these regulations and base your decisions on these. These standards/ protocols/ regulations are written and implemented to protect your client and yourself. Be honest at your workplace. Honesty and consistency are integrity.

First Paycheck: Not Really Greener Pastures?

My first paycheck was 12,000 pesos or around 300 Canadian dollars. I was part-time, on probation pay, and with heavy heart I was walking home trying to be grateful, contemplating the fact that back in the Philippines, I will earn 300CAD or more, and spend in peso. I couldn't help but compare this to my other friends who are foreignurses whose first paychecks ranged from 2,000-5,000 CAD.

But hey, I told myself, this is my first pay in three months. People back home won't know I received this pay. What they know, I guess is that once I arrived in Canada, I probably was given thousands of dollars for doing nothing. Of course, that view is wrong. I was not. You have to work more to earn more—just like in any other place.

Although, on the bright side, I don't have to pay rent since my sister and her family adopted us when we arrived. I have more time to network and learn more about Canada and the opportunities that Canada and the world can offer. With my pay rising over time, I can buy more books and learn new concepts of things. I am able to share with the groceries and buy my stuff. I am able to send money home just because we wanted to celebrate some occasions.

Patience. Canada will test your patience. If you compare yourself to others whom you think are earning more than you do, then that is the start of frustrations. I always remind myself that I chose Canada, and she doesn't owe me anything. People always ask me if I am happy to be living in Canada. I cannot answer them, especially if I consider the happiness I feel every time I go back to the Philippines. But one thing is for sure, I am grateful. Canada has opened many opportunities for me—not just to my professional self but also on my personal development.

<u>The greener pasture is where you water the grass. Rewards are not given to those who do nothing to receive them.</u>

First Day I Became A Certified Nurse in Canada (Registered Practical Nurse)

Everybody was ecstatic. I arrived May 2014, and by April 2015, <u>I had received my certificate of registration from the College of Nurses</u>. I informed my boss at work, and she was delighted. She asked me to sign another contract from them to hire me as an RPN. I was given more jobs and responsibilities. One was to help with updating the care plans.

I won't ever forget my first night as an RPN, as I had my first mortality in the retirement home. That night made me realize that a title entails a bigger responsibility. Not that being a UCP does not take away a shift without mortality, it's just that because you are legally practicing your profession, you become more conscientious.

If we talk about the pay raising after being certified, it did happen. Our income is directly proportional to the service we render and the responsibilities we take on. If we are afraid to handle more, then it is as good as saying we are afraid to receive more.

First Winter—The Season:
The Night is Long And Cold

Winter is pretty, but she's extremely cold. I personally looked forward to my first winter in the Great White North. I definitely know that Canada has snow, but nobody told me that it has lots of snow.

My first Christmas here was a wet Christmas. I thought I was doing well with winter wearing my winter jacket my uncle gave me and the warmer I wore with my pants. But here come January and February. My sister advised me to wear snow pants—a bulky, black waterproof pants. The secret to surviving winter is layers of clothes. So be it.

Either you drive your own car or not, winter is a challenge for commuters. The road is wet and slippery. As for me, who is an avid bus rider, an evening and a night shifter, I have to travel for one and a half hours from home to my first job. It takes two buses and long waits in between. If I finish at 11 p.m., I have no local bus from the main bus stop to our place. To go home I have to walk for 20 – 40 minutes, depending on how thick the snow is.

I experienced walking with the snow knee-high and windchill of (– 15). Because you are exerting effort while you walk, you are sweating and at the same time freezing. Once you remove either your gloves or toque because of your sweat, the windchill will paralyze your fingers or your ears. I have also tried to walk on a very slippery road and found that your winter boots can actually slide from one place to another. With poor balance, you will fall, and it will slide your whole body from point A to point somewhere.

Winter is also an expensive season. You have to gear up, and you have to spend money to do so, unless people will give you their old gear. If you have car, you need winter tires and other winter stuff to ensure your car is safe to drive during winter. If you have a home to maintain, the heater is always on, you put salt on your walkway to keep it from being slippery, and you have to shovel snow. You'll expect static electricity from your body, dry air, some nosebleed, and a frequent runny nose.

The whole winter experience made me a new person. Looking back (which doesn't mean I don't experience it anymore, because Canada winter is six months every year), I realized that winter is one of the challenges I agreed to face when I chose Canada. This is one of the enjoyable challenges I endure every year. Winter made me understand being Canadian, being in Canada, and being the other person that I would be capable of.

Winter reminds me that people adapt. Because if we can't, then we wouldn't survive the evolution.

First Time Being Discriminated

In five years here in Canada, I was called "a dark-skinned person" twice, and had mentioned my being Immigrant, Asian, Oriental, Filipino, number of times—but I don't mind.

My only problem exists when any of my features become the basis of my ability to do my job. For example, a client refused my care because I am a "male nurse." Some families would not ask me medical questions since I was not a certified nurse in Canada, yet. Some went looking for a "real nurse" when they realized I was an unregulated care provider. Whatever the reasons behind their doubts about my ability, it is something that I have no control over. Have I felt discriminated? Not at all. I felt more limited though to what I can do because of the perception of others. For someone who is practicing in a health profession, if your care provision is being limited because of your features, it does not help your client or yourself at all.

Discrimination exists—even in Canada, where the majority of the people are friendly. I have watched videos of one person shouting against another person because of his feats. Once I had heard the sound of it when a certain driver shouted towards us, "Brown monkeys, go back to your jungle!" It's not just me, I was one of the six people that he may be addressing. It was heavy in the ear, but I don't mind.

In general, I still believe that Canada knows no color. They treat everyone as a person, and they have zero tolerance for racism and bullying. Although there's one important thing that I want to point out on this entry: discrimination also exists in our mind.

Whenever other people called me, identified me, made fun of my accent and my practices and maybe my ideas – I acknowledged that those things are external and beyond my control. What I can control is how I respond to those external stimuli. I have met minorities that make their "being minority" a big deal. These people who always start their statement, "Just because I am 'this,' you're treating me like 'that'." I don't know, maybe there is truth in the context of their complaint, but listen, how you treat yourself, is how other people will treat you.

If you believe in your ability, you do your job well, and you respect yourself and others, I don't think the perception of others will affect you. In Don Miguel Ruiz's classic book, *The Four Agreements*, he states:

> "Whatever happens around you, don't take it personally... Nothing other people do is because of you. It is because of themselves... Even when the situation seems so personal, even if others insult you directly, it has nothing to do with you. What they say, what they do, and the opinions they give are according to the agreements they have in their own minds..."

Once we muster the ability to make things not be a big deal, we gain freedom. However, if safety is at risk and bullying and discrimination are evident and results in abuse and violence, call the authorities.

Also, discrimination sometimes comes from ourselves. We feel inferior to others because of our circumstances. Being a newcomer, having a different background, English not being our first language, and all other deep-rooted insecurities. When we limit what we can do because of our present circumstances, we discriminate against ourselves and block our potentially better self from emerging. Once and for all, this should stop. Our brain protects us so much that it can create fear for us not to explore what else we can do. If we believe what our brain says, rather than believe what our inner self says, we will be stocked.

First Time to Quit A Job

I have written in my blog about <u>how to manage doors of opportunities</u>. Clearly, Canada has opened many doors for me, and many of those I have entered. As I have written on my blog, not all doors have room for you to stay. Sometimes, you have to make a decision whether you want to stay or let go, especially if staying in the room is unhealthy for you.

I quit that job. A deliberate decision and a hard one. The best thing about growing professionally and personally is that growth actually opens more opportunities. If I were at the point in my life where I didn't have a choice but to suck it up and try harder, I'd probably stay with the expense of my health. But I know for sure that I have options. I was a newly certified nurse, an investor, an entrepreneur, and a person who seeks growth. I had a vision of how my future would look like, and if things do not match the vision I had, then I would let go.

I trust the process. I trust God. I trust my ability. Opportunities come to those who seek and to those who create it. It was still one of my best employment decisions, ever. I have learned my limitations, I have learned to accept my weakness, and I have gained the courage to risk the process of quitting.

First Leap of Faith—Going Back to the Operating Room

I was a full-time RPN nightshift in the same retirement home where I worked. For two years, it has been my comfort zone. I know and respect everybody, and they treat me the same. I am paid far more than the $300 paycheck I received on my first pay. During this time too, I was being considered to be a new Director of Care or Nursing Service Manager. I was humbled by the opportunity, but I did not take it.

I thought I was okay. I have a pretty much stable income. I know how to budget my pay. I have decided to stay put. In my mind, I am waiting or will create a big break. Whether it be in my career or business plans or just a big break, I didn't realize that I was just waiting.

A friend of mine who worked in the operating room in the Philippines asked me if I was interested in joining a course called *Operating Room for RPN*, knowing that I was an OR nurse. I had seen this course offered before, but I had not really thought about pursuing it. She told me that she enrolled in this special course and convinced me to join the class.

It was my first leap of faith after being stagnant in my career. I submitted my application and was accepted as a waitlist. Few months before the classes start, the college called me, and they accepted my application. It was a relief. Then I felt excited and anxious—I probably was doing the right thing.

Everything went well during the course. I finished with honors and was accepted to one of the best pediatric hospitals in the world, as an OR staff RPN. I didn't realize that this was going to be one of the highlights of my career in Canada. I am still waiting for another break—being a registered nurse and more personal goals to achieve.

I have always believed that when you feel comfortable where you are, it's probably a sign that you need more growth. Life is about excitement. Excitement makes us look forward to what's new in store for us. This makes us happy. Being comfortable is good, not until you lost excitement. If you ignore this itch, this will numb you. You regress.

Don't let comfort numb you. Let comfort be your driving force to seek what's more. To seek for another adventure. Don't be trapped in a wheel or a system that you doesn't even know if it's broken. Be consistent in driving your wheels. Seek for growth in every aspect of life. Because once we grow, that is the only time we can nurture others.

Good luck on working on your dreams. If you want to connect, you can always email me at chester.gonzales@foreignurse.com. Like my Facebook page "Foreignurse." Visit my blog regularly and subscribe to my vlog (upcoming).

Hope this simple guide helps you. If it does not give any value to you, I am willing to give your money back on purchasing it (and maybe a coffee meet up, too?).

Love lots,

Chester Gonzales, foreignurse

References

Catholic Centre for Immigration and LASI World Skills. (July 2012). Career Transitions Program for International Medical Doctors and International Health Professionals Client Workbook 3rd Edition. Ontario.

Gonzales, C. (n.d.). www.foreignurse.com/blog. Retrieved from www.foreignurse.com: www.foreignurse.com/blog

Miguel Angel Ruiza, M. ,. (1997). The Four Agreements. San Rafael, California: Amber- Allen Publishing, Inc.

Sovren Group, Inc. (2017). Retrieved from www.sovren.com: https://docs.sovren.com/Documents/tips-for-electronic-resumes

Wheatman, D. (2014, May 17). Retrieved from www.workitdaily.com: https://www.workitdaily.com/cover-letter-mechanics-how-to-write-a-good-one

Acknowledgement

This book guide is my first venture on self-publishing and authoring. This serves as a reminder that I can do all things as long as I am focus on achieving what my heart desires. But this would not be possible without the presence of my parents Lina and Vic. They kept me inspired amidst the challenging days we had together.

Also, I am thanking my two sisters (Ate Cathy and Ate Tin) and kids and the whole family and my brother (Kuya Chris) and kids and family and my extended family, who always believed in me.

I am also grateful to my best friend (Merwin Balmaceda) who was my critic, and who always challenge me to finish what I have started and apply what I have learned in the most annoying way even when he's on the other side of the world. Also huge thanks to Christian de Jesus who was my other critic on my book cover design, and Jessa Santos for her quick proofread of my additional notes – all for free.

Also, I would like to thank the owners of the photos I put on the first page of this book and profile picture of my Facebook page 'Foreignurse'. They are my friends and foreignurses around the globe: Ralf Aiban Alcaras (Germany), Donna Alogoc (Canada), Cham Angeles (Saudi Arabia), Merwin Balmaceda (UAE), Karen Bumatay (Saudi Arabia), John Patrick Galang (Australia), Ate Jill Pena (UAE), Edwin Punzalan (Kuwait), and Jessa and Benedict Santos (Abu Dhabi).

My other best friends from high school, college and work. The people I have met in Canada on my first year. God is great that I am blessed with beautiful people. This product is a culmination of their ideas and the experiences and learnings I have with them.

To all the nurses, dreamers, creatives who always inspire me to share my message: Thank you.

I thank God for the opportunity to share my gifts He bestowed on me. Through His grace I pray that this the start of many, and may He continuously bless me so I can inspire and help others.

About the Author

Chester Gonzales presently works as a registered practical nurse in the operating room at one of the hospitals in Ottawa, Ontario. He landed in Canada May 2014 and by April 2015 he was given the certification to practice nursing in the province. He started his job in Ottawa as a personal support worker and unregulated care provider to a retirement home. He had six years of operating room nursing experience in the Philippines before he migrated. He was the first editor-in-chief of his former hospital affiliation's nursing service publication in the Philippines. He started his nursing blog www.foreignnurse.com on 2017 to inspire all the nurses who choose to work abroad. He is an investor, an entrepreneur and a motivator. He is looking forward of becoming a registered nurse in Canada and U.S.A as an international educated nurse and publish more books. He loves travelling, and you probably going to see him wearing a cap on.

What's next?
Free Stuff to Follow your Transformation!

Please like 'Foreignurse' Facebook page and or visit my blog frequently (www.foreignurse.com) to be updated on more free giveaways to ensure your transformation to your dream job. See you in!

COMING SOON (Working Titles)!!!

From Doing your Job to Building your Life:
A Practical Guide to Investing in Yourself, and in Your Life.

From Surviving to Thriving: 100 Tips
and Stories of Nurses for Nurses and Everybody